THE

GHOSTLY TALES

OF

THE
JERSEY
SHORE

Published by Arcadia Children's Books
A Division of Arcadia Publishing
Charleston, SC
www.arcadiapublishing.com

Spooky America is a trademark of Arcadia Publishing, Inc.

First published 2023

Manufactured in the United States

ISBN 978-1-4671-9724-3

Library of Congress Control Number: 2023931847

All images used courtesy of Shutterstock.com; p. 26 EQRoy/Shutterstock.com;
p. 38 Erin Cadigan/Shutterstock.com; p. 56 Emily Pelella/Shutterstock.com;
p. 64 George Wirt/Shutterstock.com.

Spooky America

THE GHOSTLY TALES OF THE JERSEY SHORE

PATRICIA HEYER

Adapted from *Haunted Jersey Shore Beaches, Boardwalks and Lighthouses* by Patricia Heyer

arcadia
CHILDREN'S BOOKS

NEW YORK

PENNSYLVANIA

NEW JERSEY

LONG
ISLAND

DELAWARE

ATLANTIC OCEAN

TABLE OF CONTENTS & MAP KEY

The Boardwalk

Welcome to the Spooky Jersey Shore!

What do you think of when you hear someone mention the Jersey Shore? Do you picture yourself riding a wave on a boogie board, or perhaps soaking up the sun on a sandy beach? Maybe you see yourself rushing down a long wooden boardwalk with a hot pretzel in one hand and a ticket to the amusement pier in the other. You may even imagine yourself standing at the top of a lighthouse staring out to sea, to where the ocean and sky meet. These are just a few things that come to mind when we think of the New Jersey Shore.

Over the years, tens of millions of people have traveled through New Jersey because it is located at the crossroads of America. Some came during the good times of our nation's growth, and others witnessed our nation's heartbreaking tragedies. With more than one hundred and forty beaches, eighteen boardwalks, and eleven lighthouses open to the public, the Jersey Shore welcomes millions of visitors each year.

And speaking of visitors, did you know there's *another* type of tourist the Jersey Shore is known to attract? Only ... more of the HAUNTED variety? That's right. With so many people, and so much history, it should come as no surprise that this narrow stretch of sandy soil also welcomes countless ghost sightings, creepy hauntings, and many other peculiar happenings. It doesn't seem to matter if you are sitting on the beach, strolling on a boardwalk, or even climbing the staircase of a lighthouse—at the Jersey Shore, you are always surrounded by ghosts!

Hundreds of years ago, fleets of whaling ships that braved the dangerous Atlantic Ocean called the Jersey Shore their home. At the same time, lawless pirates plundered any ship that rode in with the tide, and ghostly specters from those chaotic times continue to haunt us today. These beaches have also been the site of countless shipwrecks. At night, weary phantoms roam the shore seeking rescue, completely unaware they died hundreds of years ago during the battles that raged here during the American Revolution.

Many people say that New Jersey's shores are haunted because they have a lively and colorful history, and this is why spirits have chosen to remain here. (Or maybe it has something to do with New Jersey having some of the best beaches in America.) After all, whether you're a ghost or not, everybody loves the beach life—or should I say the beach *afterlife*?

Either way, the Jersey Shore has too many hauntings to count, and visitors are almost certain to encounter something spooky, unexplainable, or downright mysterious. Many unnamed apparitions are known to linger alongside us as we explore our favorite boardwalks and lighthouses. Should you visit any of the lighthouses from Sandy Hook to Cape May, you will notice that no two look exactly alike, and each has its own unique history—very haunted history, of course!

Indeed, the lighthouses along the Jersey shoreline do have *one* thing in common:

they are all crawling with ghosts! Ghosts in lighthouses are so popular that both Absecon and Cape May claim to have the most haunted lighthouses on New Jersey's coastline. There are spirits who stay to protect the lighthouse, others who like to tease guests, and some who are just happy to call a lighthouse their home.

Within these pages, you will encounter many, *many* ghosts that call the spirited Jersey Shore their home. Look closely, and you will get more than just a glimpse of these spooky and curious remnants of the dead. That is, if you dare to seek them out!

Long Beach Island

A Ghost Asks "Why?"

Long Beach Island is a beach lover's paradise. The eighteen-mile-long beachfront boasts swimming, fishing, great food, and even pirate tours. Each year, more than a hundred thousand visitors arrive at what some people call the best summer vacation spot in New Jersey. What many people don't know, though, is that Long Beach Island is also called the most haunted island in America!

That may be because the waters around Long Beach Island are so dangerous. Underwater sandbars have caused thousands of shipwrecks along these beaches, taking the lives of thousands of sailors. Perhaps that is why they call it the "Graveyard of the Atlantic."

Today, Long Beach Island is one of New Jersey's most popular tourist spots. But at the dawn of the 20th Century, the island had a bad reputation. Pirates were known to come ashore, and smuggling was big business. At about the same time, lawless bands of thieves known as "wreckers" roamed the oceanfront, luring ships closer to the shore.

Once a ship was trapped in a sandbar, those onboard had no choice but to try to reach the safety of the beach. All the while, the gang hid in the darkness waiting for the frightened passengers and crew. Then, using a white handkerchief that had a rock tied in one corner as a weapon, the bandits struck the innocent victims, killing them instantly as they came ashore. After robbing their bodies of any valuables, the thieves left them to rot on the sand.

With such a gruesome history, it is not surprising Long Beach Island is home to countless reports of spine-chilling hauntings. It seems many of the spirits are anxious to let people know they are here.

There are reports of phantom ships and ghosts in old-time clothing along the water's edge. Even the dunes of Long Beach Island are riddled with baffling sounds and creepy shadows, as phantoms from the 1854 shipwrecked *Powhatan* roam the beach searching for their shipmates. Visitors to the shore have seen spectral images of pirates, old-time sailors, and victims of the infamous "wreckers" left to die along the water's edge.

One story from those days describes such a haunting: Walt lived on the bayside of Long Beach Island his entire life. Like the other men in his village, he worked along the waterfront all year round. In the summer, he manned the fishing boats and gathered clams. During the off-season, he scraped and repainted boats and mended fishing nets. Walt took pride in being a good neighbor and, above all, being honest and kind to others. Everyone liked him because he was always willing to help out a friend. But little did anyone know, Walt had a terrible secret that he'd come to regret forever.

Late one night, as Walt was walking along the shore, a ghost suddenly appeared before him. But not just any ghost. When Walt stared into the eyes of the pitiful creature along the beach, he knew exactly who it was—and what she wanted. Horrified, Walt quickly ran away from the shadowy creature, terrified that she would find him.

Night after night, the female specter appeared, and each time, Walt would make a mad dash for his cottage the moment she revealed herself. One night, Walt decided it was time to face his fears. He was nearly home when he first spied the ragged woman shuffling in his direction. Her eyes never left his face as she lurched slowly toward him. A small stream of dirty water dripped from her tattered clothing, and her hair fell in muddy clumps on her shoulders. Dangling from her left hand was a long white handkerchief with a rock tied in one corner. It was not until they were face-to-face that Walt saw the telltale black-and-blue bruise that covered her forehead. It was a death mark: a wound left by a wrecker who had used the handkerchief and stone to end her life. That wrecker was Walt—it was *he* who had killed her so long ago!

She raised the handkerchief toward him and whispered, "Why? I thought you were coming to help me!"

Walt tried to speak but no words came. Then, in an instant, she vanished, and Walt never saw her again. At night, he would take walks looking for the old woman, just wanting to ask: *Is it too late to say I am sorry?*

Longport Beach

A Haunted Ship on Longport Beach

Longport is a small seaside town on the southern edge of Absecon Island. It has welcomed people from around the country for decades. During the early twentieth century, Longport was famous for its hospital for sick and disabled children. Hundreds of injured World War I soldiers also spent months there recovering from their injuries. During World War II, Longport was host to the military once again, serving as a training station for new recruits. Over the years, there have been strange sightings and ghostly apparitions along the beachfront. Specters of shipwrecks, ghosts of sickly looking children, and shadowy images of wounded soldiers are common all across the area.

One interesting encounter took place just before Christmas in 1942. World War II was in full swing. Military barracks lined the shoreline in Longport. It was December 23, just two days before Christmas, and the temperature dropped to nearly zero degrees. It was already dark when the day's training ended. The troops hurried back to the warmth of the barracks for some hot chow and mail call. The men gathered behind the heavy blackout curtains, staring at the mail clerk who

was calling out names. The moment a soldier heard his name, he snatched the envelope and hurried to a corner to read.

Gary, a young private from Ohio, did not receive a letter. He had family back home, and although they wrote regularly, there had been no mail for him all week. He looked around the room at the faces of his buddies and sighed. There would be no more mail delivered before the 25th. He would be all alone for Christmas, without so much as a Christmas card from home. No one noticed that he grabbed his field coat and a knit cap before creeping out through the side door.

As he stepped out into the gloom of dusk, the dark shadows startled Gary and took him by surprise. He hurried away from the building and followed a path down to the beach, where he walked for a while along the shore. He thrust his hands into his pockets to keep them warm and turned up his collar against the frigid night air.

It was a clear night, and as Gary stared out to sea, Ohio seemed a million miles away. It was then that he noticed a murky fog forming along the surf. Suddenly, a sharp wind began to blow from all directions, and Gary struggled to stay on his feet. The swirling clouds expanded, growing thicker, and began to take form on the beach.

Gary rubbed his eyes in disbelief. He could not believe what he was seeing. He looked again, and there within the fog was the unmistakable form of a ship. But it was not just *any* ship—it was a great wooden two-masted schooner, its sails flapping wildly in the fierce breeze.

At that moment, the great ship let out a mournful groan. The wind flung it broadside into the thundering breakers. It rolled on its side and began to break apart. All the while, waves smashed against it, lifting it slightly, before shoving it back against the hardened sand. As the ocean engulfed the doomed ship, the sound of splintering wood echoed along the shoreline, as one by one the great wooden planks broke apart.

Gary could only stare in disbelief. Then his training kicked in. Why was an old sailing vessel so near to camp? Was it the enemy? Were they under attack? He raced back to camp to get help.

Crashing through the door, he shouted that a ship was sinking on the beach. At first, no one moved, then in an instant, they grabbed their weapons and headed for the shoreline.

But when they got there, the beach was empty and still. There was no wild ocean, no sinking ship, and even the crescent moon that had hung over the sea just before had disappeared.

That night was the worst of Gary's entire army career. His buddies grumbled at him for calling them out on a wild goose chase. The sergeant thundered across the beach and stood within inches of his face, demanding to know,

"Just what is going on?!" The grilling went on for hours, and although Gary insisted upon what he had seen, he still spent Christmas peeling potatoes as punishment for lying.

Except . . . it wasn't a lie. Gary had seen the ship with his very own eyes.

Hadn't he?

It was more than a month before Gary could get permission to leave the camp again. One

day, he was walking along the beach when he met an old fisherman named Gus who was well-known to the young troops at the camp. Gus had lived there his entire life, and he was always happy to share local gossip and stories with the young soldiers from his days at sea.

They talked for a while, mostly about the war, and then Gary told him about the strange thing that had happened that night on the beach. The old man threw his head back and laughed. "Did you say back on December 23? Right before Christmas? Well, son, you didn't imagine it. You saw the ghost of the schooner, *Mary Ellen*. She sank there on December 23, 1872. Hit the sandbar and sank like a rock."

Gary's eyes were wide as he caught his breath.

"Yep," old Gus said, nodding. "She comes back for a visit every now and then."

At first, Gary sighed with relief. He'd always known that what he'd seen that night was not something he had imagined. But then his relief turned to fear.

After all, if the ghost ship was real ... what *else* might be lurking in the darkness beyond the waves?

The Inn at Cape May

An Invitation
to a Haunting

The wide, sandy beaches of Cape May are lined with old-fashioned hotels and guesthouses that can make you feel as if you've gone back a hundred years in time. Visitors come all year round to Cape May. Some want to enjoy the sun and surf while others come to explore the beautiful buildings, or search the beach for quartz pebbles known as Cape May Diamonds. And many more come in search of ghosts! Not only is Cape May the oldest seaside resort in New Jersey, it is also one of the most haunted.

No matter where you go in Cape May, ghosts are the topic of conversation. Dozens of books about Cape May's hauntings fill the gift shops and bookstores. Restaurant and hotel staff happily share the latest sightings of their resident spirits. You can even take nighttime ghost walks!

Should you join a ghost tour, you may meet the ragged ghosts of shipwreck victims, ferocious pirates, or phantom bootleggers lugging great barrels of rum to shore. There are creepy ladies in white, noisy spirits in empty rooms, and even spine-chilling corpses of old-world sailors roaming the beach.

One report reveals the story

of a well-mannered ghost, who waited for an invitation before haunting a little guesthouse that sat along the beach in Cape May. Most people with a haunting in their home will tell you the ghost has been there as long as anyone can remember. But if you ask Josh and Marg—the managers of the little guesthouse along the beach—when their resident ghost first arrived, they'll not only tell you the day the ghost moved in . . . they'll tell you the *hour*!

Their ghost arrived on Christmas Eve many years ago, and has been there ever since. The haunting has nothing to do with the fact that it was Christmas Eve, other than that was the day Josh invited the ghost to supper.

Since Josh didn't believe in ghosts when he opened the small guesthouse, he had no reason to believe the old fisherman he met on the beach that day was already dead. Like many old fishermen, Ned wore an aged oilskin jacket that smelled of freshly applied linseed oil, and his frayed sailcloth pants were as wrinkled as his weathered face. But it was a friendly face, and Josh and Ned began to talk and even took a stroll along the beachfront together the first night they met.

Within a few weeks, they were meeting each evening to walk along the shore and were soon chatting like old friends. Josh talked about the

problems of running a seaside guesthouse, and Ned described his adventures as a fisherman with the local fleet.

One night, Ned asked Josh about the history of the inn and jokingly asked if they had a resident ghost like so many buildings in Cape May.

Ned's question made Josh chuckle. "No," Josh replied. "Not a single ghost. But I do admit that I often wonder why so many ghosts would choose Cape May as a haunting spot."

Ned didn't answer for a minute or two, then said in a faraway, almost wistful voice, "They're looking for a place to rest I expect . . . somewhere to call home."

Josh was surprised by the answer, but when he turned to look into Ned's face, the old fisherman was staring out to sea.

It was about the same time that Josh first

invited Ned to his house. Ned seemed nervous, and quickly answered, "Oh, no, I can't come."

But Josh didn't give up. Each week, he'd invite Ned, and each time, Ned said he couldn't make it. It didn't matter if Josh invited him for supper, or to drop in for a game of cards, or just to get together and watch a ballgame. Ned always refused. He never gave an excuse, only said that he just could not make it.

After several months, Ned had turned down invitations to barbeques, picnics, and even Thanksgiving dinner. Josh couldn't understand why Ned always refused his invitation. As Christmas approached, he became more and more determined to convince Ned to come over for the holiday celebration. But as always, each time he asked, Ned's reply remained the same: "No, I can't."

Finally, Josh couldn't hold back any longer. "Ned," he said. "I thought we were friends. Why won't you come for dinner on Christmas Eve?"

The fisherman didn't answer at first, then said, "Are you sure you want *me* to come to your house?" It was only when Josh promised he did that Ned agreed. "Okay, I'll come if you really want me to."

Josh was delighted. Each night during their walks, Josh reminded Ned that he was expected for Christmas Eve dinner at 7:00 p.m. On Christmas Eve, Josh waited eagerly for his friend to arrive. Colored lights twinkled on the tree, a fire crackled in the fireplace, and the smell of roast turkey filled the air. Josh waited and waited. But when Ned still hadn't arrived by nine o'clock, Josh knew his friend was not coming. He couldn't remember a Christmas Eve when he had ever felt so sad.

Just then, the smell of linseed oil began to waft throughout the house. Josh rushed to the front door thinking Ned had finally arrived. But there was no one there. In the morning, the faint odor of the linseed oil remained, and although he searched the entire inn, Josh couldn't find the source of the smell.

That evening, Josh rushed to the beach to meet his friend, but Ned was not there. In fact, Ned never showed up at the beach again. That holiday was the worst Josh could ever remember. He moped around the house all day and even stopped taking his nightly walks along the beach.

Back at the inn, meanwhile, the strange smell lingered. Sometimes it was so faint, Josh could hardly tell it was there at all, and other times it was overpowering. He inspected the basement, attic, workshop, and even the garage, but could not find the source of the linseed smell.

A week or two later, a guest complained to Josh about the smelly old fisherman in room four who not only came in at all hours of the night, but also *reeked* of an annoying fish-like smell. Although Josh first assured his guest they had no fishermen staying at the inn, and that room four was empty, he grabbed the key from the rack and rushed up to the second floor.

As he approached room four, the smell of linseed oil became overpowering. He unlocked the door and marched in, expecting to see an intruder. But the room was empty, with nothing out of place. As he turned to leave, though, he saw something out of the corner of his eye. In the mirror was a reflection. It was *Ned,* still dressed in his oil coat and sailcloth pants!

Josh stared at the old fisherman, unable to speak.

Ned laughed. "Hello my friend.

Why are you surprised? You invited me to your home, and here I am."

For a moment, neither spoke.

"You know," Ned said, "I would never haunt a house unless I knew I was truly welcome. You did invite me over for Christmas Eve dinner, did you not?"

At that, Josh smiled. "Of course, my friend. It's just that, well . . . I didn't know you were dead when I invited you." Then, he laughed. "Welcome home."

From then on, Josh never questioned the stories people told about their resident ghosts. Sometimes, he even shared how *his* guesthouse had come to have its very own (and very polite) ghostly guest. Other times, he didn't need to explain: at least three times a year, Ned applied linseed oil to his coat. Then, everyone knew the kind ghostly fisherman was there.

Asbury Park Convention Hall

CHAPTER 4

A Ghost With Musical Talent

Most people agree that the boardwalk is the heart and soul of the seaside town Asbury Park. People have been coming to this boardwalk for more than 140 years! Some come for the amusements and food, but most come for the music.

Asbury Park has been famous for live boardwalk music for decades. In addition to rock and roll stars, the famous Convention Hall has played host to world-famous entertainers of blues, jazz, country music, and more. Concerts have welcomed thousands to the 3,600-seat hall since it first opened in 1925.

With so many visitors, concertgoers, and rockstar legends, it's no wonder Convention Hall is also known for being one of the most haunted places on the Jersey shore. Ghost hunters and paranormal investigators have studied the hauntings at Convention Hall for many years. They confirmed the reports of visitors being touched or even pushed by unseen hands. Voices, moans, crying, and laughter are often heard there. There are sudden drops in temperature on hot summer days, new batteries mysteriously go dead, electric lights flicker off and on, and electrical devices stop working altogether. There have been mysterious shadows seen on the balcony, footsteps heard in empty halls, and, even *more* frightening, former employees (who are no longer living) are seen back at their old posts! Sometimes music will erupt from somewhere deep inside the building with no known cause—well, no *human* cause, that is.

One report came from a young man named Joe, who didn't believe in ghosts—not until he met one face-to-face. Joe took a job that summer as a night watchman at the old Convention Hall in Asbury Park. Nightshift wasn't his first choice, but it was just until school started again, and it paid pretty well. Besides, there was another kid from school working that shift, too, so at least there'd be someone to hang out with during their break. The night crew was small but friendly. They joked and laughed as they went about their chores making the night pass quickly.

Their crew was responsible for closing up the building for the night. They made certain all the guests and other staff were gone, locked the windows and doors, and set the alarms. Unless there was a special task that needed their attention, they were left to keep an eye on the security cameras, and then walk through the building every hour, checking to see that everything was in its place. This gave the crew time to get to know one another and swap stories. They talked about sports, their families, and of course, the many tales of the hauntings in Convention Hall.

Joe didn't believe in ghosts, but he always kept a smile on his face as he listened to the tales of phantom footsteps, sudden freezing temperatures in mid-July, and shadows on the balcony. Not so long ago, one of the crew claimed to have heard the old pipe organ playing during their overnight watch. But Joe had a hard time believing the tale was true. For one thing, though the pipe organ had once been so popular it was used for daily concerts (a fact that everyone found funny), it hadn't worked in *years*. For another, the base of the old building extends two hundred feet out over the surf line. The waves breaking beneath the building would bash against the floors, creating mysterious echoes and sounds filled with fright. The others might say those were "ghosts," but Joe knew better.

Or at least...he thought he did. One night, Joe arrived for work to find they were short-staffed. He would be on his own the whole shift. Joe really didn't mind being alone in the empty Convention Hall. There had been no program that day, so there was very little to do. He needed to make sure the doors were all locked and the alarm was set. Then, all he had to do was stay awake until the next guard on duty arrived.

Joe made sure the entrances were secure before he began his first walk-through of the building. Everything was in its place. The organ console was locked up tight, and all the props and equipment were stored away neatly. As Joe moved slowly through the empty building, the only sound was the clicking of his own heels on the cement floor. After a couple of laps around, he paused, and the building went quiet. Then, suddenly, a loud gust of wind broke the silence, so powerful it sounded like a giant had just exhaled! The sound startled Joe. Where had it come from?

For a moment, he stood silently, watching and listening for some kind of movement. When nothing happened, he breathed a sigh of relief and started up the balcony stairs. His imagination must have been playing tricks, he told himself. That's all.

But halfway up the staircase, the air filled with an ear-shattering bellow! Joe jumped in fear and nearly fell. At that moment, he knew he wasn't alone.

For what felt like an eternity, he stood frozen in place, listening closely. That's when the building filled once again with sound. The same wailing cry rang out, jolting Joe with fright. It was loud, powerful, and seemed to be growing *louder* every minute. But then, the single tone transformed into a melody, full and rich . . . the sound only a *pipe organ* could make!

Joe sucked in his breath, then galloped down the stairs two at a time toward the organ console. He sprinted across the floor, hopped up on stage, and ran to the console along the back wall. His eyes grew huge, and he seemed to pause mid-step. There before him, a ghostly figure dressed in a dark blazer and white pants sat at the organ's massive keyboard, his hands resting on the keys. As the organist turned to look at him, Joe saw a smile spread beneath the man's dark mustache. In the same second the two made eye contact, Joe passed out and fell to the floor.

Hours later, the next guard arrived and found Joe lying on the floor, at the foot of a closed and locked organ console. Joe muttered something about seeing someone playing the organ. But despite a painstaking search of the entire building, they found nothing out of place:

no evidence of a break-in, no damage, and—most importantly—no sign *anywhere* of the mysterious organist.

It took a long while before Joe would admit that he had seen a ghost. Although he spent more and more time there searching for the mysterious musical apparition, he never again saw the spectral organist of Convention Hall.

The Ocean City Boardwalk

The Ghostly Guardian of the Ocean City Boardwalk

Ocean City is known as "America's Greatest Family Resort," and claims to have the best boardwalk on the shore. For 150 years, the friendly beach town has offered endless family fun on its two-mile boardwalk. Here you'll find arcades, rides, gift shops, restaurants, and even a trio of theme parks. To top it off, every kind of yummy snack food you can imagine is waiting for you on the boardwalk.

Despite suffering damage from hurricanes and fires, the Ocean City Boardwalk remains one of the most popular on the Jersey shore. Tens of thousands of people visit each year, but should you visit, don't be surprised if you happen to come upon a ghost out for a walk, or perhaps a phantom anxious to entertain you!

Among the many gift shops along the boardwalk, one is home to a ghost of an old sea captain. The uninvited phantom arrived some years ago and simply refuses to leave. The shadowy figure wears a tattered

double-breasted sea captain's uniform and clutches an old wooden pipe in one hand. He arrives near closing time each day and paces back and forth looking out to sea. The captain does not speak or pay any attention to those around him.

A three-story guesthouse located on the boardwalk has been haunted for many years. The owner insists that a group of ghosts have moved into their attic and are not about to leave. The spirits never go anywhere else in the building and will not allow anyone to enter the attic. In the evenings, the shadows of the spirits are seen in the upper windows. Sometimes they try to frighten those walking on the boardwalk late at night.

For many years, the Music Pier has been one of the most popular spots in Ocean City. A variety of concerts and shows are offered each week. There are reports of unexplained happenings there, like lights going on and off unexpectedly, and apparitions trying to interrupt a show. Ghosts at the Music Pier have been known to try and take part in concerts, and sometimes will even heckle (or rudely interrupt) a performer. As if a living crowd wasn't enough pressure!

The most famous ghost in all of Ocean City is Emily. She has "lived" on the boardwalk in the famous Flanders Hotel for many years. Emily is known around the world as a happy and cheerful spirit who roams the hotel singing, laughing, and playing pranks on staff and guests. In fact, she is so popular that a huge painting of her hangs at the main entrance! Should you visit the Flanders Hotel, be sure to say hello to Emily.

Another strange tale comes from 1926, when a wind-swept fire destroyed most of Ocean City and much of the boardwalk. When the repair crews began to rebuild the boardwalk, they discovered the body of "Billy," a homeless man well-known around town. It seems he had been sleeping under the boardwalk the night of the fire and could not escape.

Frank, a worker on the boardwalk building site was troubled because no funeral was arranged for the old man. Everyone knew Billy, and Frank thought the least they could do was chip in and give Billy a proper send-off. But when he asked the other workers to donate money for a funeral, they laughed in his face.

The next morning, the workers arrived to find their worksite had been trashed. Lumber was tossed everywhere, cartons of nails were dumped on the ground, and tools were missing. The angry crew had to clean up the mess before they could even begin work.

The very next morning when the crew arrived, the site was a wreck once again. It looked like a tornado had gone through all the building materials, scattering them in every direction. The supervisor demanded to know who was responsible, but no one had a clue. The place was such a mess that the workers were sent home for the weekend.

On Monday, when the men arrived for work, they feared the worst. To their surprise, there was not so much as a nail out of place. The lumber was neatly stacked on the sand, and the tools were organized in the toolboxes. There was even the faint smell of lilacs drifting over the site. The crew was happy to be getting back to work without any more problems.

It wasn't until their lunch break that the men had time to talk about what had happened. Frank started to laugh and told them that the problem had been solved. There wouldn't be more vandalism at the worksite. Frank's boss then demanded to know how he could be so sure. With a big smile, Frank announced: "You all know the boardwalk was Old Billy's home.

I knew he wouldn't leave it, not until he had a proper burial. So, over the weekend, I helped give him a proper goodbye. I even brought him a bunch of lilacs."

The work on the boardwalk continued with no further disruption, and it was ready to reopen by Memorial Day. Now, many years later, the boardwalk continues to offer guests countless ways to have fun, yummy food, and its very own collection of ghosts. Keep an eye out—and sniff the air every now and then for lilacs—because you just might meet one!

THROUGH THIS ARCH WALK THE HAPPIEST PEOPLE IN THE WORLD

The Wildwood Boardwalk

CHAPTER 6

Watch the Tram Car, Please!

The Wildwood Boardwalk is known as the family fun capital of the Jersey Shore because there is always something fun to do. It is home to world-class roller coasters, five amusement piers, beachfront water parks, thrill rides, and tons of family fun. To top it off, popular restaurants and countless food stands fill the air with mouthwatering aromas.

Usually, people are so busy having fun at Wildwood that they don't think much about ghosts—but they *should*, because Wildwood is one of the most haunted boardwalks in New Jersey.

Many of the ghosts there don't seem to know they are dead. They show up for work and go about their business as usual. Other spirits go out of their way to let you know they are there. They make noises, move things around, and may sometimes let you see them. If someone laughed at you when you dropped your ice cream on your shoe, it just might have been a ghost having a laugh. The worker who snatched your ticket at the water slide was more likely a ghost.

One well-known haunting involves the famous yellow-and-blue "Sightseer" tram cars. Every day from 11:00 a.m. to 11:00 p.m., the singsong call, "*Watch the tram car, please,*" echoes up and down the boardwalk. The tram rattles along the length of the two-and-a-half mile walkway, just long enough for people to get off and on as they please, stopping at one attraction to the next. Thousands of people ride the battery-powered tram each year, making it one of the most popular attractions in Wildwood.

Brothers Brian and Mike were no strangers to the tram. They had been riding it each summer for as long as they could remember. It was a hot August night, and the two could not sleep. Their parents had gone to a movie and would not be home until much later. It was too dark to ride their bikes, and there was nothing on TV, so they decided to head down to the boardwalk and maybe grab a slice of pizza.

They found pizza right away, and far worse soon after. They each had two slices, then wandered down the boardwalk enjoying a bit of cooler air while watching the lights from the amusement pier. They didn't notice that much time had passed until the lights in the shops began to dim, and suddenly it was quite dark along the pier. Mike looked at his cell phone, then practically shouted, "Yikes! It's after eleven, we'd better get home!"

As Brian reached for his tram pass, Mike muttered, "Never mind, it's too late, the trams don't run after eleven. We'll have to walk." They walked for a while, but it seemed to be getting darker by the minute. "Come on!" Mike shouted, and the two began running as fast as they could toward home.

Before long, the brothers had to stop and catch their breath. They were still a long way from home, and the lights from the boardwalk were so dim they could hardly see. That was when they first felt a blast of icy, frigid air, followed by the familiar singsong cry, "*Watch the tram car, please!*"

"Oh boy, a tram!" Brian shouted. They turned to look behind them, only to see a yellow-and-blue "Sightseer" racing toward them at full speed. As it came closer, what they saw made them gasp: there was no driver in the seat of the tram!

Before either could speak, the tram hurled passed them. Then they saw a newly married couple riding in the final car. The bride's gown billowed out both sides of the tram, hiding the groom except for his red sequin jacket.

Suddenly, the wedding couple turned to look at the boys, but within seconds, both couple and the driverless tram vanished—though not before

Mike and Brian caught a glimpse of the bride's and groom's faces. They were nothing but *skeletons*! The two boys stood frozen in place, staring into one another's eyes. Neither spoke. Then, they turned and raced for home.

When they told their parents what they had seen, their folks laughed and treated it like a

joke. But Brian and Mike knew the truth. Many nights afterward, they walked the boardwalk hoping to see the haunted tram again, but they never did. Even today, the two are still careful when riding the Wildwood tram cars—making sure the tram does indeed have a driver before they hop on board!

The Sandy Hook Lighthouse

Old Fashioned Ghosts and Newfound Spirits

Way before cell phones and the internet—in the days even before Louis Pasteur discovered that germs cause illness and Edison invented the electric light bulb—the Sandy Hook Lighthouse was shining brightly on the Jersey shoreline. First lit in 1764, the nine-story white tower is the oldest working lighthouse in the United States. It stands near the tip of Sandy Hook at the entrance to the Port of New York, marking the safe passage into the harbor for ships from around the world.

The Sandy Hook Lighthouse played a key role in the American Revolution. At the beginning of the war, the American patriots tried to knock down the lighthouse to prevent the British from taking it. They

were not successful, and the British captured the lighthouse. At the end of the war, the British tried to destroy it by firing cannons at the tower. Both attempts failed, and the eight-sided tower still stands today, casting its life-saving beam of light more than nineteen miles out to sea.

To reach the top of the tower, you must climb the 199 cast-iron steps of the spiral staircase. From there, you can count the massive cargo vessels making their way into New York Harbor, or just watch the waves break on the seven miles of Sandy Hook shoreline. You can even identify famous skyscrapers in nearby Manhattan!

Today, the lighthouse is popular with summer tourists, year-round visitors who study

local history, and plenty of ghost hunters. Most people agree the Sandy Hook Lighthouse is haunted, as reports of apparitions, ghostly sightings, and peculiar unexplained events at the lighthouse have been reported for many years.

In 1860, the year before the American Civil War began, Sandy Hook Lighthouse was already nearly one hundred years old. By that time, the lighthouse and the keeper's quarters needed repair. As the workers were digging, they found an old iron door buried beneath the earth. When they finally pried it open, they found a hidden room. Inside the locked room, they found a small cot and a table with a single chair. Nearby was a small crumbling fireplace, and a skeleton sitting in a rocking chair.

No one has ever discovered who built the mysterious underground room, and the skeleton has not been identified. Also, we will never know why he was locked in the underground chamber. Are the reports of ghostly figures and unexplained noises within the lighthouse actually the restless spirit of this unknown man? No one knows, and we probably never will.

Almost one hundred years later, in 1940, the army was digging trenches for new plumbing at the lighthouse when they discovered more human remains. One woman and fourteen men were found in a single grave. But since we don't know if the remains were skeletal, mummified, or if they were decomposing bodies, we don't know when they were buried. No one has explained who the individuals were, or even, how they ended up there. Are *these* the spirits that unsuspecting visitors have met at the Sandy Hook Lighthouse? They could very well be.

There are also reports of ghosts from the American Revolution who still haunt the lighthouse. Claims of British soldiers standing guard near the base, or American Loyalists keeping watch of the tower, have been reported by visitors. Sometimes people witness ghostly soldiers firing their muskets at some unseen enemy!

Another ghost from that era is that of the American patriot, Joshua Huddy. Huddy was captain of the local militia and commanded *The Black Snake*, a private ship he used to terrorize local people who supported the British. Huddy was captured in 1872 and immediately hung. To this day, the ghost of Captain Huddy appears near the place of his death in Highlands, all across Sandy Hook, and at the top of Sandy Hook Lighthouse searching the horizon for the British fleet.

Aside from these strange beings, the lighthouse is the site of countless reports of hauntings and unexplained events. Visitors experience sudden chills on a hot day, hear footsteps on the iron staircase, and even notice a smokey presence floating along the handrails. The lighthouse staff has reported faraway voices, muddled conversations, and peculiar smells. A few insist they have been touched or pushed by something unseen. Sometimes displays in the visitor center move about, and in the offices and workrooms, things fall off desktops for no reason. The most common complaint is the feeling that someone—or *something*—invisible is watching.

One unusual haunting at the lighthouse came to light in the early 1950s, and reports of the same bizarre circumstances continue today, as this ghost seems to literally change right before our eyes. It all started when World War II ended in 1945. Although the fighting stopped in May, it took many months to bring home the nearly eight million American soldiers stationed abroad. Sandy Hook became a reception center, welcoming home tens of thousands of war-weary soldiers. Each day, ships arrived crammed with troops from all branches of the military. The one thing they had in common was that they all wanted to go home.

One of these soldiers was a young corporal from Nebraska. He had reddish hair and was named Rusty. While everyone else spent the day playing cards and grumbling about how long it was taking to get their discharge papers, Rusty always had a smile on his face. He spent his days exploring Sandy Hook. He loved to walk on the beach, collect shells, and stand watch in the lighthouse. When others complained that they wanted to go home, Rusty often replied, "I love it here. I could stay here forever." The rest of the men could never understand. But then one day, Rusty received his discharge papers, and he boarded a bus heading home to Nebraska.

Sandy Hook was a busy military site—so busy, in fact, that weeks later, no one paid attention to a young corporal with reddish hair who seemed to hang around the base with nothing special to do. He was friendly and talkative, and always anxious to show newly arrived troops around the base. He chatted with anyone who would listen about the history of the lighthouse, and once even said, "Oh, this is my home base. I want to stay here forever."

There genuinely seemed nothing suspicious about the corporal.

But as you may have guessed by now, Rusty never made it back to Nebraska. He was killed in a bus accident on the Pennsylvania Turnpike the same day he left. It seems that his ghost headed straight back to Sandy Hook, and for the next few years, there were many reports of the phantom corporal in the old lighthouse.

Since then, Rusty, the corporal ghost, seems to appear less and less each year. By the 1960s, few remained who had actually seen him. Those who had seen him claimed the corporal had not aged in the least. He was usually seen at the lighthouse, just gazing out to sea.

Today, however, reports of the corporal's apparition suggest that his appearance *has* changed. Although still visible, Rusty's ghost is now known to be pale, nearly gray, and seems to have difficulty moving his arms and legs. According to locals, he pays no attention to the living, and merely stands at the top of the tower for hours, still just staring out to sea. Many have said they've even seen a faint shadowy figure wearing a faded World War II uniform floating along the spiral staircase.

We may never know for sure if the corporal's apparition is real or imagined.

But if the ghost at the Sandy Hook Lighthouse truly is Rusty, it would seem the young soldier who once said, *I love it here. I could stay here forever*, tried his best to do just that.

Barnegat Lighthouse

Hauntings at
Barnegat Light

Ol' Barney, better known as the Barnegat Lighthouse, rests on the northern edge of Long Beach Island, where it stands guard over the dangerous shifting sands of the Atlantic coastline. Since 1859, the 162-foot red-and-white tower has weathered hurricanes, ocean storms, and even an earthquake. It has prevented hundreds of shipwrecks, welcomed millions of people to America, and guarded our shores during two world wars. Barnegat Light is just forty-four miles from the Port of New York, making it an important marker for the thousands of cargo ships that line up to insure safe passage into the harbor each year.

Today, it is one of the most photographed lighthouses in all of New Jersey. Ol' Barney is indeed beautiful, and like many of the other lighthouses along the shore, Barnegat Lighthouse has many stories of hauntings and strange happenings. You won't be able to tell the lighthouse is haunted just by looking at it. After all, it looks like any other well-kept lighthouse. There is a fresh coat of paint on the tower, and the windows are sparkling clean. Inside, there is not so much as a speck of dust, cracked brickwork, or even a cobweb to be found. The state park where the lighthouse stands is well-kept and always filled with happy visitors. But in life (and perhaps, also in death) things are not always as they seem. And sparkling clean though it may be, countless spirits call the old tower their home.

Not everyone who visits Ol' Barney is lucky enough to meet these resident ghosts, but should you be brave enough to climb the 217 steps to the very top of the tower, you just may make a new friend. You might hear the cries of shipwreck victims stranded just offshore, or meet a phantom from the American Revolution.

There are specters of old whaling ships that appear suddenly near the lighthouse, only to vanish right before your eyes. There are noises that can't be explained, and smells so strange they can't be identified. You might meet John Bacon, a spirit not to be messed with, or a pair of sad-looking phantoms searching for their baby. You may be lucky and watch as Andrew Applegate seeks revenge, again and again.

The ghost of John Bacon has been spotted

on Long Beach Island for over two hundred years. His story began in 1780, when the American Revolution was in full swing. The United States had declared independence from Great Britain and was still trying to drive out the British. Battles were being fought all across New Jersey.

One day, a small group of American soldiers managed to capture a British ship when it got stranded on a sandbar not far from shore. On board the ship, they found a large amount of food and weapons, all of which the American army needed.

They quickly began hauling it onto shore for safekeeping. Although the American soldiers worked without stopping all day, there was still more cargo to bring ashore when it became too dark to work. The men stretched out on the beach to sleep, planning to finish the job in the morning.

It was then that Captain John Bacon and his band of British loyalists came upon the men and killed them as they slept. Although Bacon was captured several months later and hanged for his crime, he swore revenge.

Now it is said that near the anniversary of this grizzly event, the ghostly image of Captain Bacon can be seen storming across the beach swinging a bloody sword at everything in his path. Those who have seen the raging captain flee in terror. (Wouldn't you?!)

Not all ghosts are as bold as Captain Bacon. Some spirits you will hear long before you see them coming. Like the young couple dressed in old-fashioned clothes. If they cross your path in Barnegat Light, the first thing you will notice is a faint jingling sound that grows louder and louder. But the phantoms are not likely to appear unless you happen to be pushing a baby stroller. Only then do they show themselves, pausing for just a moment to peek in at the baby. The jingling then stops, and the couple vanishes right before your eyes.

These specters are from the 1880s, a time when thousands of people fled a great famine in Europe for a new life in America. They hid whatever valuables they had, such as coins, jewelry, or family heirlooms, often sewn into the hems and pockets of their clothes for safekeeping.

One unlucky couple was on their way to America with their newborn baby when an ocean storm wrecked their ship near Barnegat Light. In a panic, they sent their baby to safety on the shore with the first of the rescuers. But while they waited their turn for rescue, a huge wave smashed the ship to pieces. They tried to swim to the beach, but the weight of the valuables in their clothing pulled them to the bottom. They both drowned. Now the spirits of the heartbroken couple can be spotted walking the shoreline near the lighthouse in search of their lost baby, with the sound of coins still jingling in their clothing.

Another tale from Barnegat Light is the

haunting of a former lighthouse keeper. If you wonder if a ghost could ever seek revenge, meet Andrew Applegate. He not only sought revenge during his lifetime but also continues to do it today, nearly a hundred years after his death.

Andrew Applegate may be the most chilling phantom at Barnegat Lighthouse. He was a keeper at Barnegat for many years, so it is not surprising that his spirit is still here. In fact, he died there in 1928, when he got caught in a fishing net and drowned. But the haunting at Barnegat Light by Andrew Applegate doesn't come from the way in which he died... it comes from something that happened four years earlier.

It all started one day in 1924. Andrew was head keeper at Barnegat Lighthouse. He lived there with his wife and family. One day, Andrew was working in the tower when he heard his wife screaming in terror. He raced from the tower to their living quarters, grabbing his shotgun on the way. An intruder had crept into the house and was threatening Mrs. Applegate. Andrew chased the prowler away, firing at him with his shotgun.

Now, on certain nights, Applegate's ghost can be seen once again chasing the intruder. He fires his shotgun at the fleeing figure, then chases him into the dunes. Just when it seems the culprit will escape, the scene suddenly vanishes. Often the scene is repeated two or three times like a mini movie before it vanishes completely.

So, if you visit Ol' Barney, you may be able to watch as Keeper Applegate chases away the intruder. But should you encounter Captain John Bacon and his bloody sword, well, I would *run*.

Cape May Lighthouse

The Electrified Ghost of Cape May Lighthouse

The beam from the Cape May Lighthouse stretches twenty-five miles out to sea, providing lifesaving information for hundreds of ships that pass along the Atlantic coast. Here on the southern tip of New Jersey, the red-capped lighthouse has guided whaling ships, cargo vessels, and passenger liners through these dangerous waters for more than one hundred-sixty years.

When the Cape May Lighthouse was built in 1859, it was built to last. The Army Corps of Engineers, who built the tower, began by creating a stone platform that reached twelve feet down into the earth. This solid base allowed the lighthouse to withstand the strongest storms and remain intact, despite the weak sandy soil of the area.

Then, to be sure the tower was strong enough to survive hurricanes, they built the tower in two separate layers. The round inside layer is made of brick, which supports the great spiral staircase. The outer layer is shaped like a cone and is made of masonry, which withstands wind, rain, and saltwater spray. On the top, they placed a deep- red twelve-foot cap made of metal and glass. From there, visitors have an amazing view of Cape May, and the overhead flashing beacon can be spotted twenty-five miles out to sea.

Although Cape May Lighthouse is known for being one of New Jersey's most beautiful tourist attractions, it is also known as one of the most haunted lighthouses on the New Jersey shoreline. There are nighttime ghost tours, full moon tower climbs, and even a trolly to carry you to and from the lighthouse. No wonder thousands of people visit the lighthouse each year hoping to meet ghosts!

The many different kinds of ghosts you may meet at the Cape May Lighthouse might surprise you. There are ghosts that try to let visitors know they are present by touching them or making sounds. Other phantoms do not seem to know they are dead, and others repeat the last few minutes of their lives over and over again. There are spirits of the children who once lived there, and even a few ghostly pets of former lighthouse keepers. Within the lighthouse, there are apparitions from the days of the great whaling ships and the shadows of former keepers and their families.

One female spirit dressed in old-time clothing is often seen lugging a bucket of oil up the spiral stairs. Although she climbs the staircase day after day, she never seems to reach the top of the tower. Another ghost hovers on the third landing unable to move

upward or downward. There is a weeping phantom surrounded by a group of ghostly children. Sometimes the haunting is replaced by an unruly ghost racing up and down the spiral staircase, searching for something unseen. Spirits of children are heard laughing or seen chasing one another across the grounds. Yet other ghostly toddlers are heard crying, or sometimes reaching out to touch visitors. Many guests report feeling an icy cold chill within the tower, even on the hottest summer day.

One well-known haunting at the lighthouse is that of a former keeper named Samuel Stillwell. Captain Stillwell, an American Civil War hero, served as head keeper at the Cape May Lighthouse for more than twenty-five years. He was in charge in 1891 when a bolt of lightning struck the lighthouse during a thunderstorm. The lightning hit the dome and then traveled down through the tower into the keeper's quarters. The damage was so serious that Keeper Stillwell and his family had to live in temporary quarters for seven months while their home was repaired. Ten years later, lightning once again struck the lighthouse. This time not only were the keeper's quarters damaged but the young daughter of the assistant keeper was seriously burned.

After that, Captain Stillwell kept a constant eye on the weather. Whenever a thunderstorm approached, he immediately evacuated the lighthouse. Just a single clap of thunder would send the no-nonsense keeper into a frenzy, ushering both staff and visitors away from the tower.

Now, many years later, the ghost of Keeper Stillwell appears in the lighthouse whenever a storm comes near. He races up and down the spiral staircase, urging visitors to leave the tower at once. It has been said that he will give a gentle shove to anyone who lingers.

Once he has cleared the tower, Captain Stillwell's ghost keeps staring at the sky. Then, as the storm moves in, he stands outside in the downpour, steering the lightning bolts away from the lighthouse. Some say his ghostly figure can be clearly seen at the *exact* moment the lightning bolt strikes.

The loyal keeper remains there to this day, protecting the lighthouse whenever a storm is near. Captain Stillwell's spirit reminds us that although Cape May Lighthouse is beautiful, it is no place to be during a thunderstorm.

Absecon Lighthouse

CHAPTER 10

The Camera-Shy Ghost of Absecon

Absecon Lighthouse is not only the tallest lighthouse in New Jersey, but also claims to be the most haunted. Although many people enjoy the view from the 171-foot tower, many others come just to take the daily ghost tours. It seems everyone wants to climb the 220-step spiral staircase to the top of the lighthouse, hoping to meet one of the *dozens* of ghosts that call the tower home.

In fact, there are so many stories of spooky happenings at the Absecon Lighthouse that it is hard to keep count. Eerie voices, unexplained footsteps, and hair-raising screeches are often heard. Doors open and close for no reason. Ghostly figures in torn and frayed uniforms from the American Revolution are seen floating at the base of the tower.

Moaning specters wander from room to room inside the keeper's building in the early morning hours. Inside the tower, ghoulish faces float across the interior walls. Visitors have been frightened by the sight of a single human hand sliding down the handrail of the spiral staircase. As if this were not enough, the smell of cigars can be so strong that workers must turn on fans to clear the air.

Just this summer, it was revealed that one of the best-known ghosts at the lighthouse refuses to be photographed. You might not think a ghost would mind having its picture taken. But in this case, he minded very much.

It was just getting dark when a car with out-of-state license plates pulled into the parking area at the Absecon Lighthouse. The family had planned to arrive in time to climb the tower, but the traffic had been heavy. They could tell the moment they pulled into the lot they were too late. The lighthouse was dark and deserted, with only the "closed" sign visible at the entrance.

Just then the door opened, and a tall lanky tour guide stepped outside. He turned and looked at them, then smiled. At first, they didn't see anything unusual about him. Except for the fact that he was extremely pale, and his clothes appeared to be at least twenty years out of date, he looked like an ordinary tour guide.

When they asked about the lighthouse tour, he looked at his watch and shook his head. "I'm so sorry, the official lighthouse tours end at five o'clock, and it is nearly *six* o'clock." When the younger child began to cry, the tour guide looked as if he might cry as well.

"Well, I could give you a quick tour myself, if you like," he said. "After all, you did drive a long way just to see the lighthouse. Come on, follow me." The grateful parents quickly dug into their wallets, but again, the guide shook his head. "No, money is not accepted on this tour. This is a special nighttime visit," he announced with a giant grin.

They all introduced themselves as they hurried toward the entrance. The guide told them his name was Ambrose but said they could call him "Brosie." The children laughed at his funny nickname, which made the tour guide smile from ear to ear.

He led them to the entrance of the lighthouse tower and then stopped dead in his tracks at the door. He turned around and whispered to the children, "It's after hours, we really shouldn't be here." His eyes sparkled in the dim light as he added," Besides, the tour is *always* more fun in the dark." Before they could answer, he handed each one a small flashlight. "Here," he said. "They are a little dim. These batteries never last long for some reason. But I think they will do."

The family followed the guide into the darkened lighthouse. At first, their flashlights seemed to light the way, but the farther they went into the tower, the fainter the lights became. Brosie never stopped talking. He described how the lighthouse had been built back in 1854, told stories about some of the former keepers, and even shared a ghost story about the famous lighthouse.

Suddenly he shouted, "Follow me!" and bolted up the spiral staircase to the first landing. The family hesitated for a moment, then began their trudge up the steps one at a time. Each time someone stepped on the metal stairs, a dull clanging sound echoed off the walls. After they reached the first landing, the climb seemed easier, although it got darker and colder with every step upward. The children were giggling about the cold, but Brosie didn't seem to notice.

When they finally reached the top of the tower, the

spectacular view made the whole family gasp. On one side, the colorful lights of Atlantic City glittered in the darkness. On the other, it was pitch dark, with only the lighthouse's golden beam shining miles and miles across the inky sea. The view was so mesmerizing that for a long time, no one said a word.

After a bit, the guide said it was time to go, so they began their long trip down the spiral stairs. Their flashlights were useless by then, so they moved slowly and carefully in the dark, everybody feeling for the next step with their foot before they moved farther. They finally reached the bottom, and before they knew it, were back outside.

Brosie said goodbye and was about to leave when the parents asked if they could photograph him with the children. At that, Brosie's smile became a deep frown. He explained that he never permitted anyone to take his picture and turned to walk away.

"*Please?*" the children begged, chasing after him. "Just one picture?"

He sighed as he looked into their pleading faces. "Okay," he agreed. "But just one."

They all gathered together near the base of the lighthouse. Brosie stood in the very middle, with the happy family gathered all around him. The father held out a selfie stick, counted to three, and took the picture. At the exact moment the camera flashed, the tour guide instantly bolted away from them. When they looked up, it was as if Brosie had vanished into thin air.

The family stared at one another. Where had he gone? They scrolled through the phone until they found the picture. There was the family gathered together at the base of the lighthouse, but in the very center where the tour guide had stood ... there was only a grayish cloud.

They had met Ambrose, the well-known, camera-shy ghost of Absecon.

A Ghostly Goodbye

Now that you've walked with us down the piers and climbed the tallest lighthouses of the Jersey Shore, do you think this is a place you'd like to visit? Are you confident the lost ghosts pacing along the shores and hiding in the dunes are going to be friendly to you? Or maybe you still don't believe in ghosts, even after everything you've read here. Well, that's okay—but fair warning: if you find yourself surfing with a specter along the Jersey Shore, just remember: *we told you so!*

Patricia Heyer is a local history buff with a special interest in New Jersey folklore and marine science. She has written extensively for both children and adults during her career. Her most recent title, *Haunted Jersey Shore Beaches, Boardwalks and Lighthouses* was released in 2022. Pat is an avid reader, beachcomber, and animal rescue supporter. She resides on the Jersey Shore with her husband, Rob, and their rescue cat, Gracie.

Check out some of the other *Spooky America* titles available now!

Spooky America was adapted from the creeptastic *Haunted America* series for adults. *Haunted America* explores historical haunts in cities and regions across America. Here's more from the original *Haunted Jersey Shore* author Patricia Heyer.